STOP W.

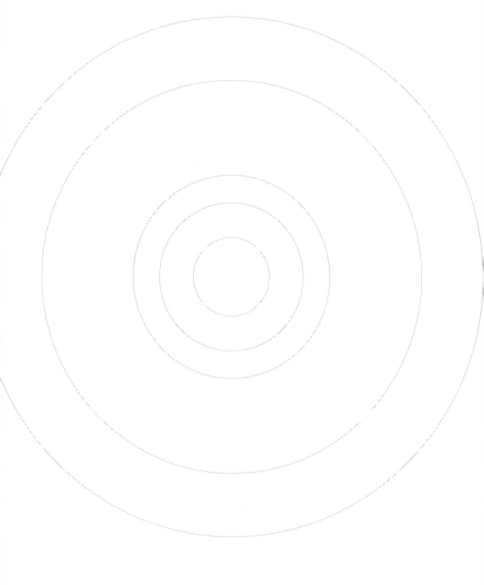

CLEVELAND STATE UNIVERSITY POETRY CENTER
NEW POETRY

Frank Giampietro, Series Editor

Michael Dumanis, Founding Series Editor

Samuel Amadon, *The Hartford Book*
John Bradley, *You Don't Know What You Don't Know*
Lily Brown, *Rust or Go Missing*
Elyse Fenton, *Clamor*
Emily Kendal Frey, *The Grief Performance*
Lizzie Harris, *Stop Wanting*
Rebecca Hazelton, *Vow*
Chloe Honum, *The Tulip-Flame*
Rebecca Gayle Howell, *Render / An Apocalypse*
Lesle Lewis, *A Boot's a Boot*
Dora Malech, *Say So*
Shane McCrae, *Mule*
Helena Mesa, *Horse Dance Underwater*
Philip Metres, *To See the Earth*
Zach Savich, *The Firestorm*
Sandra Simonds, *Mother Was a Tragic Girl*
S. E. Smith, *I Live in a Hut*
Mathias Svalina, *Destruction Myth*
Allison Titus, *Sum of Every Lost Ship*
Liz Waldner, *Trust*
Allison Benis White, *Self-Portrait with Crayon*
William D. Waltz, *Adventures in the Lost Interiors of America*
Jon Woodward, *Uncanny Valley*
Wendy Xu, *You Are Not Dead*

For a complete listing of titles please visit
www.csuohio.edu/poetrycenter

STOP WANTING

Lizzie Harris

Cleveland State University Poetry Center
Cleveland, Ohio

Published by the Cleveland State University Poetry Center
2121 Euclid Avenue, Cleveland, Ohio 44115-2214
www.csuohio.edu/poetrycenter and is distributed by
SPD / Small Press Distribution, Inc. www.spdbooks.org.

ISBN 978-0-9860257-6-1

First edition

Library of Congress Cataloging-in-Publication Data

Harris, Lizzie, 1987–
[Poems. Selections]
Stop wanting / Lizzie Harris. – First edition.
pages cm. – (New Poetry)
"Distributed by SPD / Small Press Distribution, Inc."–T.p. verso.
ISBN 978-0-9860257-6-1 (acid-free paper)
I. Title.

PS3608.A78319A6 2014
811'.6–dc23

2013049456

Acknowledgments

Grateful acknowledgment to the editors of the journals where versions of some of these poems appeared: *Barrow Street, Painted Bride Quarterly,* and *VICE.com.*

Much appreciation to Meghan O'Rourke, Deborah Landau, Sharon Olds, Lynn Emanuel, Jeff Oaks, and Breyten Breytenbach for their guidance and encouragement. Thanks to my friends at the NYU MFA, particularly Ben Purkert, Jen Levitt, Cat Richardson, Amy Meng, Emily Pan, Julie Buntin, and Andrew Eisenman for their edits and support. Thanks to the Cleveland State University Poetry Center for just being the best, especially Frank Giampietro for his insight and positivity. Thanks to my family and friends for everything else.

to Danny and Lilah, for giving me the window seat

Contents

3

4

STOP WANTING

Mythology

1

I want to say what happened
but am suspicious of stories. I can try
to write the bones from my finger,
the spine of the act that bleeds out like a cut
beneath the tongue. I want this

to be a stranger's soft tissue,
sun-shrunk to a pebble.
I need someone to look in the face of
the pond and see something
other than swans,
see how with only a mouth
I found water in a desert.

2

I was shipwrecked   yes   lost
in water   held down
by my collarbone   I was ink
woven to a man   pinned
to his body   I was water-
lunged   ocean-eyed   shoved
like a message   *Do what you want*
I'm too afraid to say   gagged at the mouth
    wrist tied to man's huge skin   thin-
skinned   vein-grown   sprouting
from the nail-beds   rooting
in the sea-bed   inked
on an inner thigh   inked   as in red-written
wrapped in a message   growing in a bed
pinned   to a body   of water
rising   in the bottle   yes   I was
shipwrecked   foundered   found in glass

3

Yes, I was a drought fire,
a small coffin filled with eyes,
then ants, then nothing.

I was bare
like a palm covering
the throat.

Had they known *they must
have known*
I could have grown
giant-sized, buildings
at my ankle.

Instead I was that coffin, sealed
and translucent. Restless,
then frantic, then nothing.

4

At eight I lost my body,
spent a decade
building a soft model
with bones made from straw wrappers. I tried
to bleach the teeth. I tried
to coat the stomach.

If I did escape, my mind escaped.
If my mind escaped, it must have flown.
If my mind flew, then it was a swallow:
a larynx choking on marrow. A swallow,
yes — fine-necked, sound-sparse.

Until It Roots

Take the body.

Bury it.

Roll the body to show the face, let it see above.

If a man holds up a fist to you, pretend to drop the shovel.

Hide your body from the storm clouds, find the richest soil.

Ask: *What should grow from this?*

Geranium will sprout from the mound, flower with earlobe,
petal like eyelids.

Whisper to the body, you are the last thing that soul hears.

Make the body a promise:

You'll be buried in the ground where no one can touch you.

Don't lie to the body: *No one will touch you again.*

Nation

We are children of the abandoned airport—the stretch
of black in the desert's throat, where mobile
homes gum at cinder blocks. In Sells,

the res is wrapped
in barbed wire, car bodies
rusting in the sun. We grow a lawn of dirt,

seed bamboo to save us
from neighbors whose walls
shriek howling. Our father builds tin

sheds and fills them with empties,
their folded gold glinting.
There are other children—a baby

girl from his new O'odham wife, her two sons—
we call each other family, sleep three
to a bed. There's P.O. boxes closer

to town. There's a Basha's you could get to
by car. There's a blacktop runway where pilots
took off to break the sound barrier.

In summer, we ride bikes
across the desert's tar tongue,
our outside toys scorching, untouchable.

We eat butter sandwiches,
we drink Orange Drink from a Looney Tunes jar.
One winter my father finds turquoise

blooming underground. He calls me at my mother's
to say it's poison to touch, but I had to see
how it veined the earth.

Long After You Were Gone,
I Just Kept Talking

In the mouth of the desert
my mother's burning cholla.
She's trying to tell me
something about eventual
forgiveness—her hand
is lit with cholla, the dry stalks
smoking neon. In the dream's
morning, char-sand rises
in the windows. It strikes me
that my mother is sleeping
in my father's bed.
I have never seen her wake to my father
cooking eggs, cracked shells
heaping in a bowl.
I can see inside my mother
to her waiting belly, the imprint
of a scooped child she cradles
in sleep, sees through
the eyes of cholla. She's dreaming
of having me or some yellow
fire to wrap herself in, build me
like a ragdoll—neon
where my face was, cholla
where my mouth was, shell
where my tongue was.

Timeline

A tar-fingered pilgrim, my father
finds the res. He digs canals
in the desert, meets my mother
at a party.

She was passed me—like a football.
She was past me, like an anchor.

She would say I was the green sign
pointing to the east, but when I left
her body, she wore me
like a leash.

There's No Other Way to Say This

At school I discovered the heart
of a white rhino, showed
my teacher with words
which were never
any use to me. I tried
to tell my mother, but
she was deaf as women
are when baking
salt cookies slipped
into a sandwich bag.
It was a fear of waking in hide.
At eight she lost
her father when the pilot
lost his radio and the sky lost
his plane. I thought
to give her my childhood: that stick
in a stick-pile, that spot
on the moon.

Wanting

[   ] rumored my body

[   ] clucked hens from my throat

[   ] passed me in the supermarket

[   ] didn't look twice

[   ] blamed my thighs

[   ] answered all of my calls but one

[   ] rooted a fern in the telephone

[   ] slugged *anger anger*. . . in slime

[   ] left me like a dress in my father's closet

[   ] manned my fingers

[   ] opened so quietly you woke in the elevator

Swan Princess, 1994

My father flew to Philadelphia, just once.
Booked a room in an old hotel with narrow halls
where he showed me the door handles, said they were broken
grips of a butcher knife.

My two siblings
and I were always stitched tightly,
but he made this trip
singular, planned a night
alone with each of us.

First was my brother, who warned
that they mostly stayed in the hotel,
exploring the space in the basement's gut.

The next night my sister was taken to wash
his laundry—forgetting I was the daughter
who loved machines.

On the third night, it's almost funny how I walked
to his rental car and found him
perched in the driver's seat, chain-smoked
while my mother was bone-locked at home.

On our drive, he was kind, smirked
we can do anything. Practiced
for autumn's ear, a wider silence.

      I must have slept
      in his hotel bed. I must have eaten.
      I must have gotten into, then out of,
      his shower.

I know he was close in the dark
movie theater where a girl hid
in the body of a swan.

For years, that night sparkles
like the shell of a mussel,
the easy memory of love. But if I follow
the long string of logic, the glow
darkens to a clot.

I'm ready to know, but
the shell won't open.
It hangs like an eyelid of stone.

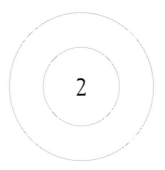

2

Erasure of a Self Help

I

Feel dirty [ii]

[iii] if people knew

they'd [iv]

Hate [v] you [vi]

[vii]

perfect

[viii]

feel [ix] [x]

[xi]

[xii] shame[xiii] feel

[xiv]

Dead inside[xv]

[xvi] Alternate

[xvii] [xviii]

nightmares[xix] [xx]

[xxi] or [xxii] Have a

hard

[xxiii] [xxiv]

[xxv] [xxvi]

on and [xxvii] feel

numb

[xxviii] [xxix]

[xxx] [xxxi]

when people get close[xxxii]

[xxxiii] Expect them [xxxiv]

II

Sitting in the tub and crying for my mother [2] I shoved my finger through my fist and said *as many times as he wants* [3] Deep sore, still touched, finger abandoned inside my body [4] See S, see C, see E, see J, see J, see J [5] Check [6] Skittish as a trash cat [7] My father, my friend's father holding a banana standing in the doorway [8] Sand-stuck, desert-skin, burning like a rug-burn [9] Check [10] When was I seven? [11] Where was I eight? [12] Check, check, check [13] Sham of the shower where I felt the spout with my big toe [14] In my head when he gripped me, his new wife, she saw it [15] On the phone in the waiting room [16] Surely have the pill bottle, always have the pill [17] Grab me from the brush, bite him on the hand [18] My front is to the window, my back to the booth [19] Teeth out—said he'd pull my teeth out with his bare hands [20] Check [21] Checked in for two weeks [22] Chest peeled, ripping off the stomach [23] Your skin, smoke skin, loose skin of the knuckle [24] Hadn't found that body [25] Hadn't found a pulse [26] A foot in hand, breast in a pocket, knee cap in a tea cup [27] Too weak, too small, joint-popped, stone-boned [28] Check [29] On the bus, in the train, saw each man with a pistol [30] Never in my sleep clothes [31] Check [32] See Z, see S, see J, see T, see A, see [33] Check [34] See check

White Loss of Forgetting

       I remember the touching
was softer than I wanted
and after   I wanted things quiet
because I didn't trust the skin
that skinned my little body   I don't want to be vague

he had my body run the water
he took my body for a carpet
he took my body from men
      I would one day want to love me
I don't want to be vague

My mother took my body to the doctor
                           she said I was infected
                           from sitting in the bathtub
but it makes a kind of after-sense
because   I was tired
of that shower reassembling my body
in steam   I had never before
seen my father in water   so perhaps
he mistook me for a spout
with a head that clicks to expose
infinite pressure   I don't want to be vague

awful things happened
the worst sinks beneath
my eye   until I can only see
my crown   I only see

my father coaxing
at the spout   but my body is small
and then it all gets

lower   and then I swear
he pulls a red thread
from my middle   and I'm so low now
I see myself from the nosebleeds
see sky like a bed   to hide beneath
                    please
                    believe me

Birdie makes mistakes,

all sorts of mistakes, so many
everything notices—the trees,
grass, angle of the dumpster—she never
comes out right. So maybe she flies right
into an oven or the sky. Some girls
have just enough to fly across an ocean
then die with a frantic heart—but still
they knew there was land to land on.
Birdie heard there was a rabbit in the moon,
that once you see it you can't un-see. Birdie sees
bad from above, recalls something cold,
but the year is so long
maybe winter was a thought she had
last time she was scared or pitied, and pity
is a kindness, a kind of lilac
orbiting a bruise. Bird can fold in memory
the zigzag of an egg in two pieces.
She can fill half with anything.

Birdie's got a chicken finger,

her feathers stacked in saucers.
Once she turned trash into a nest, just *POOF*.
You heard Bird right
                              down to her skyline.   Cut to Birdie,
who fidgets with a flight pattern. *Please keep your wings*
inside the vehicle. Please keep your eyes out
for insects glassing in amber.
                          Which moments froze?
Even ice could be a diamond if people weren't so quick.
So many things pretty,
but are just too hard to touch. Bird touched
a cloud once, the idea of one.   OK, so no one's asking
Bird for her brainwaves—you couldn't
pick her from a V.   Birdie can't find
her features, can't fine-tune her feathers.
Bird wants no piece of preening, no part
of the ground. Here's Birdie, dense enough
to land or land   or land on legs.

Bird on the ground, repeat

Birdie's on the ground: she always is.
Her chest shrinks,   her head grows,   she sees sky
and wants to bury it.   People keep leaving
because on this old earth there's too little to talk about.
Birdie's a bore,   just ask her
how many girls live inside

                            their bodies, anyway?
People say girls elevate the garbage.
Birdie chugs wine by a hydrant.   She eggs
a neighbor's car. Birdie's got good
on her shoulders, she couldn't hurt
a fly,   but who even notices her
down here with all these   leaves
blowing around.

What if Birdie is a word

for asking breath to leave a body?
How hard-headed is the right girl
                    asking the wrong question? Or,
is one Bird's trash another Bird's
larynx?   *SHHH.*   A wise Bird's whistling
don't get too close to your feathers,
you leave them.   Or they just don't hang
right. And when'll she admit she's just a little
different, just a little seed glued to a button.
Bird springs on a bullseye, lands
on a sidewalk square. Bird keeps
bread crumbs under her Bird tongue.
Bird could swallow a shoehorn
to stretch herself thin.   Go on, ask her
to skirt the asking.

Mother on the Highway

In the car my mother aimed for the median
cried for time to ungrow me or herself
said I multiplied   without her asking
          but in ways I was asked   to graph mishaps
that brought her to my father
                    who mistook me for my mother
                                        and handled me
my mother thinks I misremember
but her voice was a longhorn   and yes I knew   we were sitting in the car
                              but I felt
                                        knelt down
mouthing some holy prayer   pleading
with this woman who carted me   like a ghost in her brain
then belly
                    but she wanted me in pieces
                              she could hold again   at the wheel
she was a pilot
                              kept her own father's crash in the rearview
her car was a household   time machine
she would trade   the daughter she woke to
for her own young self
          as she liked to remember it

Stop Wanting

But what if I had wanted to be loved?
Or my mother
in her infinite fear
had tossed me into a jar
and buried me so deep in the desert
I drowned.

I don't want to forgive,
it's become a sort of closeness.

When I look back at my father,
he's a much larger man than anywhere
I could almost live. I could almost live

inside the distance stretched
between his heart and hairline—
who knows what starts the body going,
who knows what a body can take?

I couldn't take anything,

like my mother braiding my hair
tight into a fishtail, loose into
a pumpkin. Weren't we easy?
Weren't we touching on the little things?

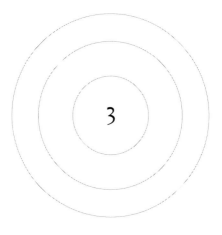

3

Body Clicks a Turn Signal

the bus was cold
then wasn't

the carpet seats
never touched me

I never saw a bridge but
the hills were ahead

then weren't
each man was armed

each man's arm
had my neck and it looked

nothing like dancing and
men might never touch on me

I was afraid of my body
which nobody waited for

a little like a bus inching
closer now to a Volvo

in the next lane the family
I imagined is listening

to voicemails the family
I imagined says will you

look outside
will you look how the sky looks

My Father as a Child Went Looking

He wanted to see the bog,
but what happened, happened

beyond it. There were two boys,
he knew them. Stood as one forced another

down below the vines and the smaller boy's mouth
fastened. He saw how timing could save

and almost did. He wanted to walk the bog,
see how the ice cranberried in winter.

But he saw the boys and ran to them.
Saw the large boy thaw

then zip his pants. The two hinged
like a knuckle in his hand.

Rough Chronology

i

I was dreaded
like a deadline, a thin string
tying her to death.

Her body made a scratching post,
a melon cut through
at the button, inside
a collection of seeds.

How much smoother would she be
had I not formed like a naval mine
floating in her womb?

I didn't know, I didn't know.

ii

She tells me there were flowers
but I know there were no flowers.

Says: *I would chop the onion;*
you would grate the cheese.

At night, I smell only the metal
of the buckle, metal of blood.

At a glance, it pools—poppies
sprouting from the tiles,

bruises are bulbs
planted just beneath the skin.

iii

You do learn the measure
of how a father spoils a daughter
and how he beats his son. He cracks

her skull against her sister's,
his thick grasp on the shortest
hairs. But a boy who can twist

his child-fist might get stomped
in his neck, tiny as a stem.

iv

Our mother strapped us on a plane—my siblings
and I, all younger than five—and it did feel
strange to fly
knowing what landscapes sprawled
between the bodies that made me.

There was a woman once,
in wax paper, wrapped in the cupboard
of my chest. She teaches me
to hide without hiding the heart.

v

On that evening,
the evening was strange.
How long had I waited
beyond the glass door? Until steam
blinded me, my esophagus
a pin-prick.

Shower, if you were here
today—if I knew where
to find you—I would climb inside
alone, also leave alone.

I would hang my arms
from the towel hooks. I would rest
my throat in a dish.

vi

A dish breaks in the kitchen:
my stepmother is screaming and flying
for the smallest corners.
Linen closet. Cactus garden.

At once, she is no longer a jewel,
a teenage girl who grew
his child in a stomach.
Now, she is a wasp nest
hiding between my legs—*hide*

hide—wait for the sound
of fists against a body.

vii

A year ago I'd have thought myself a crocus
now I'm an old mop leaning in tin

    Can you keep this thing quiet?

Teeth are collecting in my hands

    Can you   keep quiet?

Mouth is empty tasting marrow

viii

Skin is my father's
and I do not fit.
It is too large and hangs
a loose sweater
off the smaller bones
of my cheek and jaw.

It is warm and smells like desert.
It's burnt and tastes like smoke.

I think then
of my father
waking to find
his body sealed
in my young skin,
wrapped so tight
he can almost breathe.

ix

Mother,
there are days when you, soaking
in the tub, are not so far away.

I traced the stretched skin
of your abdomen with my little index finger
and asked *How old were you when I did this?*
Or, *How old when Lilah was born?*
Your answers grew thinner
at my one day being that age
with a child, a husband.

It was then you said a woman's body
could be broken into and I was sure
you meant *out of*—

Who Walks Through

Some days the door opens
like a game show door
to household goods, shiny appliances
I want to live inside—
the oven that burned me, the shower
that took me.

I want to keep machinery
closest to the door.
I want to know the ghost, cook it
in my kitchen.
I want to love people whose fingers
flip knobs in my body.

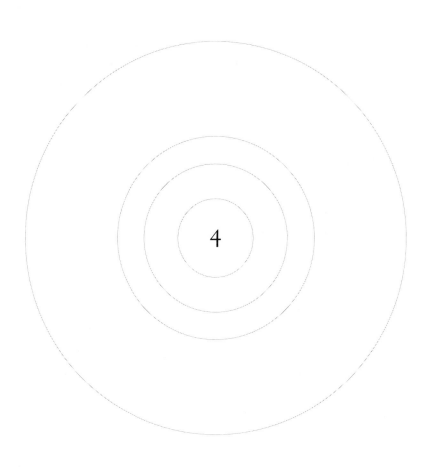

House Fire

Each house was the body of a woman
who rearranged furniture
like blood or thought or terror
and terror was a man
who barked at everything.

My mother was the dog
who loved and loved each man
more, but kept my father
like an electric collar. Fire was a teacher

who guided me through creatures—
the smaller the scorpion, the more you shake
your shoes. My mother fanned
and fanned each flame, offered me
as timber. My body was lumber,
memory the lighter.

Parents in Unadjoining Rooms

I've heard my mother took hits
like a fighter, stole three children
from a man who was one slug after another.

My father would lean into the lawn
furniture, fume about men—
you can't leave your daughter alone
in a room with one—but his anger sat
less like an apology, more
a room's largest clock. And if anger

were a knife, who could even hold it?
Who rested it in the blue-tile kitchen
lodged in my mother's ear? My mother knows

forgiveness—how a dandelion seeds
before you plant it—but I think
of her shipping me to my father, how
she held me loosely when I came back
thin and death-scared, with my hands
cupping a shield over the opening of my body.

Ugly things happen when we love
outside ourselves. A fever spreads
before you touch it. I never told
my mother. I needed her to know.

Nausea as My Father's Voice

I lived each year as an emptied stomach:
      I vomited in the grass
      on a short road trip north,
      I vomited on my body at night.

I lived each year as a bathroom lock:
      I am the queen of sliding bolts,
        the queen of stalls.

I was dry as raw coal heaving in the bowl.
I was nausea like a knuckled tongue.
Nausea spoke: *I liked you best*
when you were sick, I liked you best
quiet.   Childhood as a haiku:
      Pill in my hand fell
      to a floor of small stones, now
      I must look for it.

Inside Voice Outside My Skin

Seed of wanting, maybe
you're a coin. I just know you grow jealousy.
I'm jealous of every woman with a face.
I'm afraid to face the quiet, and if silence
cracks through me, I'll be afraid again.

I am afraid for my father to know my address,
I'm afraid he doesn't care. I'm afraid
there's a man somewhere who could love me
and I won't have the stomach for it.

Whatever's inside of me is only getting bigger:
the weight of value, the quick thought I have none.
I'm afraid that her hair is the hair you saw
in the sun that day. I put ads in the paper

that say *I'm afraid*. I play with your voice
like a loose tooth I run my tongue across,
but I'm afraid I've only made it looser.

Love Found You in a Line

and wanted to service you Love noticed little things Love took eleven days to call Love told a ghost story that made you see love clearly for the first time Love danced to Bobby Darin with his tongue out Love was a warm wet place for critters to live so warm the pests laid eggs Love untied a tourniquet Love was salt on a mango Love packed a large duffle with doorknobs but Love never asked you to carry it Love crawled to his side of the bed Love washed your dishes Love's hair was black marbles you found mango on Love's tongue you found he found you upsetting Love was a carry-on you wanted close but Love moved his body to the couch moved his clothes to the chair moved time to reveal a picture of skin Love isn't asked to disassemble anything Love made home too homely Love made impossible to make Love became invisible Love didn't answer

Want Stopping

For a moment I was a woman
whole as a watermelon   sweet
on a man who wore loafers   I told him
every story   spoke explosions
with my hands   he listened
he chewed my food so I had no use
for a stomach   but I'd wanted to digest
things   thousands of southern birds
dropping from the sky   sky changing
to a new sort of blue   like the blue
could be an eye
we want what we want
in the bedroom my stomach pulsed
like lungs   the bathroom tile
honeycombed white where porcelain
cracked a face I thought was king   excuse me

my brain's an overloaded
elevator I've filled with ten different versions
of you
one when we met   four of you sleeping
three   of you speaking
two of us in the kitchen   and
I'm so blanched with blue now

how was I as meek as a penny in your loafer
how did I stroll without a spine or pulse
for a moment I was a train-car   the landscape
paned me   with you moving tall
as trees   please   I miss your jaw
resting on my shoulder
cup in saucer
man that I love for a moment love me

I Insert My Father's Face into
Everyday Scenes

I do see you in the jaw
of each man chewing, giving
themselves like silence at a breakfast table

and once you told me I knew nothing
when I said Danny made better eggs
than you ever could

girls just don't know eggs
but food would dodge
your teeth, the whole world

skittish of your hand,
which holds and roughly
holds like you taught me

to want things that don't
want me—frantically regret
each street I don't walk on—

if the past loosens,
I'll picture you coolly, laughing
to a waitress in no particular city.

Reservation's Landscape

I've seen in a palm
who I could have been   swollen
in Arizona dry heat   scorpions
for fingers   my hair in wisteria
knots   gutting green pepper   picking
            at the chandelier of seeds
in the desert I saw beds
                                        on wheels   staying
how strange
                    to spend your whole life waiting
for the heart   only to find
                                cactus figs
rolled in sand

Crawler Perched on a Spoke

How long will you live
like mud-cake?
How long will you live?

Not long I've hoped forever I've thought.

I've thought of you
as dead already, wondered who
you speak to on the days
when I don't speak to you.

I've thought of your calls
with friends—who are they?
I've thought of the box they'll
bury you in. How I'll know its wood grain
closer than I knew you.

Tell Me One Thing Good

When I was a small thing
I couldn't sleep.
I could never sleep and my father
would take me from my crib.
He would hold me in one hand
at the curve of his neck—more the base
of his shoulder—and like cargo, I'd listen.

And my father would take me
from the house to the garden of cholla
and prickly pear, and he would tell me
everything he knew about growing.
And like a soft cabbage
I would listen.

Stop Wanting

Maybe it's wrong to want for things,
but I wanted to be a woman who flipped beauty
like a wrestler. I wanted to see men open up
after great and terrifying haircuts.

I was born on a runway desert,
in a constellation of mobile homes, old bones
of an airport. I wanted a body: soft fruit
to grow a skin around. In the desert
I wanted water, wanted bad to stop wanting me.
I wanted some alarm to sound
around my body. I sagged, wearing my brother's

green jeans. I wanted to be a boy
or to find myself closed. Is it strange to want
the past like too many hairs clinging in a drain?
Memory is kind, spares me this one time.

Waking

Rose of my eye rose where my eye was

in my ear's bud you whisper
please be less giving please
                              have more give

I will never forget you won't let me

There's Grass Somewhere,
But I Don't Know How to Find It

And if I'm wrong, what blue pulse
would darken? For years I went not knowing
why I spoke to water, why my fork stitched lace
over every plate. What thing did you water
to make me love like a socket? I do knit bricks
around my stomach, a stray licking itself sour.
As a child I lived like a crumb beneath the cushion,
now I wear pity like a dinner napkin. There are people
in this room who don't want me.
I know them.
I must have been a girl someone spoke to—I knew
each word that left the mouth. You're sure I love

for the utility, but show me an oven who doesn't
love her baker. Believe me. My first love was yellow
gloves my mother wore to wash dishes. I won't ever
be this young again. My mother still calls to say she made
my bed, each month she airs dust off the linen.
She lasts like breath in a stone lung,
but I could live one day, if or when
I'm ready to.